The Art of True Healing

The Art of
True Healing

by
ISRAEL REGARDIE
Edited and Updated by
MARC ALLEN

THE CLASSIC WISDOM COLLECTION
NEW WORLD LIBRARY
SAN RAFAEL, CALIFORNIA

Original version © 1932 Dr. F. I. Regardie
This edited version © 1991 Marc Allen

The Classic Wisdom Collection
Published by New World Library
58 Paul Drive, San Rafael, CA 94903

Cover design: Greg Wittrock
Text design: Nancy Benedict
Typography: Wilsted & Taylor

Library of Congress Cataloging-in-Publication Data

Regardie, Israel.
    The art of true healing / by Israel Regardie ;
  edited and updated by Marc Allen.
p.   cm. — (The classic wisdom collection)
ISBN 0-931432-76-6 (alk. paper)
1. Mental healing.   2. Meditation.   I. Allen, Marc,
1946–
II. Title.   III. Series
RZ401.R37   1991
615.8'51—dc20   91-21732
                                       CIP

First printing, October 1991
ISBN 0-931432-76-6
Printed in the U.S.A. on acid-free paper

"These are the methods by which the dynamic nature of the subconscious can be stimulated so that the human personality becomes transformed into a powerful magnet attracting to itself whatever it truly desires or is necessary to its welfare . . . ."

—Israel Regardie

Contents

Publisher's Preface

Life is an endless cycle of change. We and our world will never remain the same.

Every generation has difficulty relating to the previous generation; even the language changes. The child speaks a different language than the parent does.

It seems almost miraculous, then, that certain voices, certain books, are able to speak to not only one, but many generations beyond them. The plays and poems of Shakespeare are still relevant today—still capable of giving us goose bumps, still entertaining, disturbing, and profound. Shakespeare is the writer who, in the English language, defines the word *classic*.

There are many other writers and thinkers who, for a great many reasons, can be considered classic, for they withstand the test of time. We want to present the best of them to you in the New World Library Classic Wisdom Collection. Even though these writers and thinkers lived and wrote many years ago, they are still relevant and important in today's world for the enduring words of wisdom that they created, words that should forever be kept in print.

Shakti Gawain
Marc Allen
New World Library

Introduction

I discovered *The Art of True Healing* about twenty years ago, and it has been my constant companion ever since. As soon as I did the Middle Pillar meditation, I had no doubt that every premise of the book, and every promise of the book, was true—and, as you will see, the book deals with not only physical healing, but healing every aspect of our lives. Dr. Regardie says it best:

> These are the methods by which the dynamic nature of the subconscious can be stimulated so that the human personality becomes transformed into a powerful magnet attracting to itself whatever it truly desires or is necessary to its welfare. . . .
>
> Perhaps sickness is present. Or we need money. Or we have undesirable moral or mental traits—or what not. We

can elevate our minds, utilizing this energy, so that the desire of our heart automatically realizes itself with practically no effort at all. . . .

This is a bold premise, and a great promise. In my experience, he delivers on his promise. The original subtitle on the title page describes this book as "A Treatise on the Mechanism of Prayer, and the Operation of the Law of Attraction in Nature." Though the wording seems a bit bulky for today's standards, the meaning of the words is profound and powerful. Through the exercise in the book, we turn prayer—or any wish for any improvement in our lives or the lives of those dear to us—into a powerful instrument for change.

Once you try the Middle Pillar meditation, once you experience its effects, you will probably agree with me that true magic actually exists—and each of us can be a magician, and a healer, capable of improving our lives and the lives of those we love.

Of course, as Dr. Regardie himself states, these exercises are in no way a substitution for competent medical care or therapy, if necessary—but they are a wonderful addition to it, for they are able to aid the healing process in a great many mysterious, profound, and positive ways.

I do the Middle Pillar exercise several times a week, and have modified it somewhat over the years in a way that works for me. I encourage everyone to try the exercise, and to feel free to modify it in any way they wish. I firmly believe that it has definitely contributed to my health, success in the world, and ability to help others. Besides, it's a great excuse to stay in bed for another fifteen or twenty minutes, and still feel that you're doing yourself and the world a favor.

Marc Allen
Editor

1

The Force of Life

"Each one of us can begin the process of reconstruction for ourselves; each one of us can discover the force that can bring us true healing of our bodies and minds."

Within every man and woman is a force that directs and controls the entire course of life. Properly used, it can heal every affliction and ailment we may have.

Every single religion affirms this fact. All forms of mental or spiritual healing promise the same thing. Even psychoanalysis and other forms of therapy employ this healing power: The insight and understanding that effective therapy can bring releases tensions of various kinds, and through this release the healing power latent within and natural to the human system operates more freely.

Each of these systems tries to teach its own specialized methods of thinking or contemplation or prayer that will, according to the terms of their own philosophies, renew our bodies

3

and even transform our whole environment. Very few of these systems, however, actually fulfill in a complete way the high promises they have made. There is little understanding of the practical means whereby the spiritual forces underlying the universe and permeating every cell of our bodies can be utilized and directed toward the creation of a new heaven and a new earth.

Naturally, such an ideal is impossible for *all* of us to achieve without the universal co-operation of everyone. Nevertheless, each one of us can begin the process of reconstruction for ourselves; each one of us can discover the force that can bring us true healing of our bodies and minds.

The crucial question, then, is how are we to become aware of this force? What is its nature? What is the mechanism whereby we can use it?

A great many different systems have evolved, widely differing processes by which we may discover the presence of such a power. Meditation, prayer, affirmation, invocation, emotional exaltation, and other forms of declaration made at random upon the universe or the Universal Mind are a few of the methods. All have this in common: By turning the fiery penetrating power of the mind inward upon itself, and exalting our emotional system to a certain pitch, we may become aware of previously unknown currents of force, currents that are almost electric in their interior sensation, and that are healing and integrating in their effect.

It is the willed use of such a force that is capable of bringing health to body and mind. When effectively directed, it acts like a magnet: It attracts to every one of us who employs these methods just those necessities of life, material or spiritual, that we urgently require or that are needed for our further evolution.

The fundamental, underlying idea of the mental healing system is this: In the ambient atmosphere surrounding us and pervading the structure of each one of our body's cells is a spiritual force. This force is omnipresent and infinite; it is present in the most infinitesimal object as it is in the most proportion-staggering far reaches of the known universe. It is this force which is life itself.

Nothing in the vast expanse of space is dead. Everything pulsates with vibrant life; even the subatomic particles of the atom are alive.

The force of life is infinite; we are saturated, permeated through and through with this spiritual force, this energy. It constitutes our higher self, it is our link with Godhead, it is God within us. Every molecule of our physical system is soaked with the dynamic energy of this force; each cell in our body contains it in abundance.

When we consider this force, when we become aware of it, we are then brought face to face with the enigmatical problem underlying all disease: If we are permeated with this energy, and if this energy is limitless, how can we become depleted of this healing energy, and become unhealthy and sick?

What is fatigue? How can there be depletion of our energy if vitality and cosmic currents of force pour through us daily, saturating our mind and body with power?

Primarily, it is because we offer so much resistance to its flow through us that we become tired and ill. The conflict finally culminates in death.

How does humankind manage to defy the universe? How are we able to offer resistance and opposition to the very force that underlies, and continually evolves in, the universe?

There are many causes of this resistance to the inward flow of the spirit: Most of us were raised to be complacent and confused and even cowardly from childhood on into adulthood, and most of us have a false perception of the nature of life. The fact that this is generally unconscious doesn't matter—are any of us really aware of all the involuntary processes going on within us? Are any of us conscious of the intricate mechanism of our mental processes, and of the processes by which our food is assimilated and digested, and our blood is circulated, bringing nourishment to every cell?

All these are purely involuntary processes, just as, to a large degree, our resistances to life are purely involuntary. We have surrounded ourselves with crystallized shells of prejudices and ill-conceived versions of reality; we have shielded ourselves with a mental armor so dense it affords no entrance to the light of life that surrounds us.

No wonder we become sick, impotent, helpless, poor! No wonder the average individual is so unable to adequately deal with life!

The first step towards freedom and health is a conscious realization of the vast spiritual reservoir in which we live and move and have our being. When we make repeated mental efforts to make this part and parcel of our outlook upon life, part of the hard inflexible shell of the mind breaks down and dissolves. And then life and spirit pour abundantly. Health spontaneously arises, and a new life begins as our point of view undergoes this radical change.

Moreover, it appears that we create an environment in which we attract just those people who can help in various ways, and the things we have longed for manifest in our lives.

The first step is a purely mental one, involving a change in our perception of life, so that we realize we are in the midst of a vast reservoir of healing energy. The second step lies in a somewhat different direction: It involves learning a process of regulated breathing—quite a simple process, and, as you will see, quite an effective one when used repeatedly.

If life is all about us, all-penetrating and all-pervasive, what is more reasonable than that the very air we breathe from one moment to the next should be highly charged with vitality? To best take advantage of this, we need to take the time periodically to regulate our breathing in a calm, simple way, and to contemplate that life is the active principle in the atmosphere.

We should practice this rhythmical breathing at fixed periods of the day, and there should be no strenuous forcing of the mind, no overtaxing of the will. All effort must be gentle and easy; then skill is just as easily obtained.

Let the breath flow in while mentally counting very slowly, one . . . two . . . three . . . four. . . . Then exhale, counting the same beat. It is fundamental and important that we should maintain the initial rhythm that we have started, whether it be at a four-beat count or a ten-beat count or any other convenient one. For it is the very rhythm itself which is responsible for the easy absorption of vitality from without, and the acceleration of the divine power within.

Unchanging rhythm is manifest everywhere in the universe. It is a living process whose parts move and are governed in accordance with cyclic laws. Look at the sun, the stars, and the planets. All move with incomparable grace, with a steady, inexorable rhythm. It is only humankind which has wandered, in its ignorance and self-complacency, far from the divine cycles of things. We have interfered with the rhythmic process that is inherent in nature. And how sadly we have paid for it!

In attempting to attune ourselves once more to the intelligent spiritual power functioning through nature's mechanism, therefore, we attempt, not to blindly copy, but to intelligently adopt her methods. Your periods of rhythmical breathing should be at certain fixed times of the day when there is little likelihood of disturbance. Cultivate above all the art of relaxation. Learn to address each tensed muscle from toe to head as you lie flat on your back in bed. Tell it deliberately to loosen its tension and cease from its unconscious constriction. Think of your blood flowing copiously to each organ in response to your command, carrying life and nourishment everywhere, producing a state of glowing, radiant health.

Only after these preliminary processes have been accomplished should you begin your rhythmic breathing, slowly and without haste. Gradually, as the mind accustoms itself to the idea, the lungs spontaneously will take up the rhythm. In a few minutes it will have become automatic. The whole process then becomes extremely simple and pleasurable.

It is difficult to overestimate the importance or effectiveness of this simple exercise. As the lungs take up the rhythm, automatically inhaling and exhaling to a measured beat, they communicate it and gradually extend it to all the surrounding cells and tissues. Just as a stone thrown into a pond sends out widely expanding ripples and concentric circles of motion, so does the motion of the lungs. In a few minutes, the whole body is vibrating in unison with their movement. Every cell seems to vibrate sympathetically. And very soon, the whole organism comes to feel as if it were an inexhaustible storage battery of power. The sensation—and it *must* be a sensation—is unmistakable.

Simple as it is, the exercise is not to be taken lightly or underestimated. It is upon the mastery of this very easy technique that the rest of this system stands. Master it first. Make sure that you can completely relax and then produce the rhythmic breathing in a few seconds.

2

Awakening Our Energy Centers

"Most prayer and contemplative methods unconsciously employ these inner centers. We would be wiser and far more efficient to deliberately employ this spiritual power and the centers it flows through."

The next principle we must consider is fundamental and highly significant. It is the inability to realize or thoroughly to have grasped its importance that underlies the frequent failure of many different healing systems, whether physical, mental, or spiritual. Just as there are specialized organs for the performance of specialized functions in our physical body, there are also corresponding centers in our mental and spiritual nature.

Just as the teeth, stomach, liver, and intestines are mechanisms devised and evolved by nature for the assimilation and digestion of food, there are similar centers in the other components of our nature. The mouth receives food, digestion occurs in the stomach and small intestines, and there is an apparatus for rejecting waste products. In our psychic nature also are focal centers for the absorption of spiritual power from the universe without, and there are other centers for its distribution and circulation.

The dynamic energy and power entering us from without is not uniform or alike in its vibratory rate. It may be of too high a voltage, so to speak, for us to readily endure. Within us, therefore, is a certain psychic apparatus whereby various cosmic currents of energy may be assimilated and digested, their voltage becoming stepped down or adjusted to the human level. The process of becoming aware of the psychic apparatus, and using the energy it generates, is an integral part of this healing system.

Most prayer and contemplative methods unconsciously employ these inner centers. We would be wiser and far more efficient to *deliberately* employ this spiritual power and the centers it flows through.

There are five major spiritual energy centers. Since we must name them and identify them in some way, let me give them the most noncommittal and noncompromising titles imaginable, so that no system of prejudice may be erected upon them. For the sake of convenience, we may name the first one Spirit, and the succeeding ones Air, Fire, Water, and Earth.

The diagram illustrates the concept, showing the position and location of the centers. It is important to understand that these centers are *not* physical in nature and position—though there may be parallels with our physical organs and glands. These organs exist in a subtler spiritual or psychic part of our nature. We may even consider them, not as realities themselves, but as symbols of realities—great, redeeming, and saving symbols.

Under certain conditions we may become aware of them in very much the same way that we may become aware of different organs in our physical bodies. We often speak of reason as being situated in the head, emotion in the heart, and instinct in the belly; there exists a similar natural correspondence between these centers and various parts of the body.

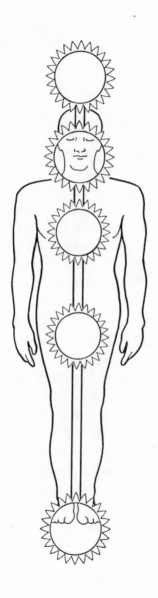

There are three principal means for us to become aware of these centers, and awaken them from their dormant state so that they may function properly. The means are thought, sound, and color. First, through our thoughts, we concentrate on the assumed position of these centers, one by one. Then we make the sound of certain names, which are to be considered as corresponding vibratory rates to be intoned and vibrated. Finally, each center is visualized as having a particular color and shape.

The combination of these three things gradually awakens the centers from their dormant states. Over time, they become stimulated, each functioning according to its own nature, and they pour forth into the body and mind a stream of highly spiritualized energy and power. Ultimately, when their operation becomes habitual and stabilized, the spiritual power they generate may be directed by will to heal various ailments and diseases both of a physical and a psychological nature. It can also be communicated to another person by a quiet, focused laying on of hands. And by simply thinking, with intent and focus, the energy can also be communicated from mind to mind telepathically, or transmitted through space to another person miles away—for objects in space cause no interruption or obstacle to its passage.

First of all, the position of the centers as shown in the diagram must be memorized. They are then to be stimulated into activity while either sitting upright or while lying down flat on the back in a perfectly relaxed state. If sitting, the hands may be folded in the lap, or they may rest comfortably on the thighs, palms upward. If lying down, your hands should rest comfortably at your sides, palms upward. Calmness of mind should be induced, and several minutes of rhythmic breathing should result in the sensation of a gentle ripple playing over the diaphragm.

Then imagine there is a ball or sphere of brilliant white light above the crown of your head. Do not *force* the imagination to visualize the sphere of light, for this only results in the development of neuromuscular tension, and defeats our end. Let it be done quietly and easily. If the mind wanders, as indeed it will, wait a moment or two and gently lead it back.

At the same time, vibrate or intone a sound. You have several choices here:

1. You can simply hum a pitch that seems to resonate, as closely as possible, in the light of your center. Or you can resonate the pitch in your throat center, and direct it mentally to the center of your choice.

2. You can intone the word from the Judaic-Christian mystical tradition that is appropriate to that particular center. For the first center, the word to vibrate or intone is *Eheieh*, pronounced *Eh-heh-yeh*. (We'll discuss these words in more depth in a moment.)

3. You can chant an English equivalent of the ancient word. For the first center, the words to chant are *I am*.

4. You can meditate upon each center, and discover the words or sounds that have power and meaning for you.

After a few days of practice it will become quite easy to imagine the name vibrating above the head in the so-called Spirit center. This name, this center, is the indwelling and overshadowing divinity in each one of us, the basic spiritual self that we can all draw upon. *Eheieh* means literally *I am*, and this center represents the *I am* consciousness within.

The effect of mentally directing the vibration to the Spirit center is to awaken the center to dynamic activity. When once it begins to vibrate and rotate, light and energy are felt to emanate downwards upon and into the body. Enormous charges of spiritual power make their way into the brain, and the entire body feels suffused with vitality and life. Even the fingertips and toes react to the awakening of the coronal (Spirit) sphere by a faint prickling sensation at first being felt.

If you're intoning a word or a name, rather than humming a pitch, the word or name should be intoned during the first few weeks of practice in a moderately audible and resonant tone of voice. As skill is acquired, then the vibration may be practiced in silence, the name or words being imagined and mentally placed in the center. If the mind tends to wander, the frequent repetition of the vibration will be a great help to concentration.

Let the mind rest in the light of the Spirit center for five minutes or so. Let it glow; feel its dynamic energy. Then imagine that it emits a white shaft downwards through the skull and brain, stopping at the throat. Here it expands to form a second ball of light, which includes a large part of the face, up to and including the eyebrows. If the larynx is conceived to be the center of the sphere, then the distance from it to the cervical vertebrae at the back of the neck will be approximately the radius. Naturally, this dimension will vary with different people.

We name this sphere the Air center, and a similar technique should be applied to this center as to the previous one. It should be strongly and vividly formulated as a pulsing sphere of brilliant white light, shining and glowing from within.

The name to be vibrated here is *Jehovah*

Elohim, pronounced as *Yeh-hoh-vah Eh-loh-heem*. Or you can use the words *I speak*. Or meditate upon that center, and make up your own words. Or simply hum into that center's radiant light.

The traditional names for the centers—*Eheieh*, *Jehovah Elohim*, and so on—are in reality the names ascribed in various parts of the Old Testament to God. The variety and variation of these names are attributed to different divine functions. When acting in a certain manner, God is described by the biblical scribes by one name. When doing something else, another name is used, one more appropriate to the actions or states of being that are represented or described.

This system has its roots in the ancient Hebrew mystical tradition. Its innovators were obviously people of exalted religious aspirations and genius; their work transcends time and even all the wide varieties of religious and philosophical beliefs. For our purposes, no religious connotations whatsoever are implied by the use of these biblical divine names. Anyone may use them without subscribing in the least to the ancient religious views, whether he or she be a Jew, Christian, Hindu, Buddhist, atheist, or anything else.

This is a purely practical, empirical system that is successful regardless of the skepticism or faith of the operator. Today we may consider these sacred names in an entirely different and useful light: They are keynotes of different components of our nature, doorways to so many levels of that part of the psyche that is usually subconscious. They are vibratory rates or symbolic signatures of the psychophysical centers we are describing. Their use as vibratory keynotes awakens into activity the centers with which their rate is in sympathy, and conveys to our consciousness some recognition of the many levels of the subconscious spiritual side of our personalities. The actual religious significance of these names does not concern us, nor do their literal translations.

Let us focus again on the Air center in the throat, and let the vibratory sounds be intoned a number of times, until its existence is recognized and clearly felt as a definite sensory experience. There is no mistaking the sensation of its awakening. About the same length of time should be spent here, and in the following centers, as was devoted to the contemplation of the Spirit center. Once this period of time has elapsed, let it, with the aid of the imagination, thrust a shaft of light downward from itself.

The light descends to the region of the solar plexus, just beneath the sternum or breastbone, and the shaft expands once again to form a third sphere. This is the position of the Fire center.

The allocation of fire to this center is particularly appropriate, for the heart is usually associated with the emotional nature, with love and the higher feelings. The diameter of this sphere should extend from the front of the body to the back. The name to vibrate here is *Jehovah Eloah ve-Daas*, pronounced *Yeh-hoh-vah Eh-loh ve-Dah-ahs*. Words to vibrate here are *I love*.

Take care that the intonation vibrates well within the white sphere. If this is done, a radiation of warmth will be felt to emanate from the center, gently stimulating all the parts and organs around it.

Since the mind functions in and through the body, being coextensive with it, the mental and emotional faculties likewise become stimulated by the dynamic flow of energy from the centers. The seemingly solid barrier between our conscious and subconscious minds, an armored partition which impedes our free expression and hinders spiritual development, slowly begins to dissolve. As time goes on, and the practice continues, it may disappear completely and the personality gradually achieves integration and wholeness. Genuine health spreads to every function of mind and body, and happiness follows as a permanent blessing.

Continue the shaft downwards from the solar plexus to the pelvic region, the region of the generative organs: the Water center. Visualize here, too, a radiant sphere of approximately the same dimensions as the higher one. Intone here, too, a name that produces a rapid vibration in the cells and molecules of the tissue in that region: *Shaddai El Chai*, pronounced *Shah-di El Chi* (the *ch* is guttural, as in "loch"). The words to intone here are *I create*.

Let the mind dwell on the sphere and the words (or pure vibration, if you choose) for some minutes, visualizing the sphere as a white brilliance. Each time the mind wanders from such a brilliance, as in the beginning it is bound to do, let it gently be coaxed back by repeated and powerful vibrations of the name or words or tone you associate with the center.

It may be feared that this practice could awaken or stimulate sexual feelings and emotions unnecessarily. For those who are feeling sexual conflicts, for any of a number of reasons, such an apprehension may be legitimate. Actually, however, the fear is groundless: The contemplation of the Water center as a sphere of white light connected by a shaft to the higher centers acts more as a sedative than as a stimulant. And, in point of fact, sexual stimulation can be very effectively dealt with, not by narrow-minded and shortsighted repression, but by the circulation of such energies through the system by means of this practice. A thoroughgoing and far-reaching process of sublimation, almost truly alchemical in effect, may be achieved. (This is not, however, to be construed as encouraging the avoidance of dealing effectively with sexual problems, through whatever form of therapy is necessary.)

The final step is to visualize the shaft descending once more from the reproductive sphere, moving downward through the thighs and legs until it strikes the feet. There it expands from a point approximately beneath the ankle, and forms a fifth sphere. We have named this one the Earth center.

Let the mind visualize here exactly as before a brilliant dazzling sphere of the same size as the others. Vibrate the name *Adonai ha-Aretz*, pronounced *Ah-doh-ni hah-Ah-retz*, or use the words *I bless*. Spend several minutes awakening this center by fixed and steady thought and by repeated intonation, then pause for a short while.

Try to clearly visualize the entire shaft of silvery light, studded as it were with five gorgeous diamonds of incomparable brilliance, stretching from the crown of the head to the soles of the feet. A few minutes is usually enough time to give reality to this concept, and bring about a vivid realization of the powerful forces which, playing upon the personality, are eventually assimilated into the psycho-physical system after their transformation and passage through the imaginative centers. The combination of rhythmic breathing with the willed visualization of the descent of power through the light shaft or Middle Pillar, as it is also called, produces by far the best results.

As skill and familiarity are acquired in the formulation of the centers, an addition to the technique may be made. Earlier I remarked that color was a very important consideration in this technique. Each center has a different color attribution, though it is wisest for a long period of time to refrain from using any other color than white.

To the Spirit or coronal center, the color white is attributed. It is the color of purity, spirit, divinity, and so on. It represents, not so much a human element, but a universal and cosmic principle overshadowing the whole of humankind. As we descend the shaft, however, the colors change.

Lavender is attributed to the Air or throat center, and it represents particularly the mental faculties, human consciousness as such.

To the Fire center, red is an obvious association.

Blue is the color referred to the Water center; it is the color of peace, calmness, and tranquility, concealing enormous strength and virility. In other words, its peace is the peace of strength and power rather than the inertia of mere weakness.

Finally, the color referred to the lowest center of Earth is russet, the rich, deep color of the earth itself, the foundation upon which we rest.

SPIRIT CENTER
White

I AM
Eheieh

AIR CENTER
Lavender

I SPEAK
Jehovah Elohim

FIRE CENTER
Red

I LOVE
Jehovah Eloah ve-Daas

WATER CENTER
Blue

I CREATE
Shaddai El Chai

EARTH CENTER
Russet

I BLESS
Adonai ha-Aretz

From this brief and concise summary, it can be seen that each of these centers has an affinity or sympathy with a different spiritual component. One center is sympathetic to or is associated with the emotions and feelings, while another has a definite intellectual quality. It follows logically, therefore—and experience demonstrates this fact—that stimulating these centers and gradually bringing them into a state of balance and equilibrium evokes a sympathetic reaction from every part of our nature. And where disease manifesting in the body is directly due to some psychic maladjustment or infirmity, then the activity of the appropriate center must be considered as affected somehow in an unhealthy way. Its stimulation by thought, sound, and color tends to stimulate the corresponding psychic principle and thus to disperse the maladjustment. Sooner or later a reaction is induced physically in the disappearance of the disease, and the consequent building up of new cells and tissues: the manifestation of health itself.

3

The Art of True Healing

"Although I have stressed the healing of physical ills, it cannot be insisted upon too strongly that this method is suitable for application to a host of other problems . . . whether it be a problem of poverty, character development, social or marital difficulties—in fact any other type of problem one has."

Now we're ready for another very important stage in the development of the Middle Pillar technique. Having brought power and spiritual energy into the system by means of the psycho-spiritual centers, how best are we to use it? That is to say, use it in such a way that every single cell, every atom, and every organ becomes stimulated and vitalized by that dynamic stream?

To begin with, we throw the mind upward to the coronal sphere again, and imagine it to be in a state of vigorous activity. It revolves rapidly, absorbing spiritual energy from space about it, and transforming it in such a way

37

that it becomes available for immediate use in any human activity.

Imagine then that this transformed energy flows like a stream down the left side of the head, down the left side of the trunk and the left leg. While the current is descending the breath should slowly be exhaled to a convenient rhythm. Then slowly inhale, and imagine that the vital current passes from the sole of the left foot to the right foot, and gradually ascends the right side of the body. In this way it returns to the source from which it was issued, the coronal center, the human source of all energy and vitality, establishing a closed electrical circuit.

Visualize this energy flowing within the body rather than traveling around the periphery of the physical body. It is an interior psychic circulation rather than a purely physical one.

Once this circulation is firmly established by the mind, let it flow evenly to the rhythm of the breathing for some seconds so that the circuit has been traversed about half a dozen times—or even more, if you wish. Then repeat it in a slightly different direction. Visualize the vital flow as moving from the coronal center above the head down the front of the face and body. It turns backwards under the soles of the feet and ascends up the back in a fairly wide belt of vibrating energy. This should also be accompanied by a slow, steady exhalation and inhalation of breath, and should continue for at least six complete circuits.

The general effect of these two movements is to establish in and about the physical form an ovoid shape—shaped somewhat like an egg—of swiftly circulating substance and power. Since the spiritual energy dealt with by this technique is extremely dynamic and kinetic, it radiates in every direction, spreading outward to an appreciable distance.

It is this radiation that forms, colors, and informs the ovoid sphere of sensation that is not limited to the shape or dimension of the physical frame. General perception and experience has it that the sphere of luminosity and magnetism extends outward to a distance more or less identical with the length of the outstretched arm. And it is within this aura, as we may call it, that the physical person exists rather like a kernel within a nutshell.

Circulating the force admitted into the system by these mental exercises is tantamount to charging it to a considerable degree in every department of its nature with life and energy. Naturally this is bound to exert a considerable influence, so far as general health is concerned, upon the enclosed "kernel" within.

The final method of circulation resembles the action of a fountain. Just as water is forced or drawn up through a pipe until it jets up above, and falls in a spray on all sides, so does the power directed by this last circulation. Throw the mind downward to the Earth center, and imagine it to be the culmination of all the others, the receptacle of all power, the storehouse and terminal of the incoming vital force.

Then imagine that this power ascends, or is drawn or sucked upward by the magnetic attraction of the Spirit center above the crown of the head. The power ascends the shaft until it surges overhead with a marvelous fountainous display and falls down within the confines of the ovoid aura.

When it has descended to the feet it is again gathered together and concentrated in the Earth center before it surges up the shaft again.

As before, the fountain circulation should accompany a definite rhythm of inhalation and exhalation. By these means, the healing force is distributed to every part of the body. No single atom or cell in any organ or limb is omitted from the influence of its healing regenerative power.

Once the circulations are completed, let the mind dwell quietly on the idea of the sphere of light, spiritual and vital and healing, surrounding the entire body. The visualization should be made as vivid and as powerful as possible. The sensation following the partial or complete formulation of the aura in the manner described is so marked and definite as to be quite unmistakable. It is marked by an extreme sense of calmness and vitality and poise, as though the mind was placid and still. The body, completely at rest in a state of relaxation, feels in all its parts thoroughly charged and permeated by the vibrant current of life. The skin over all the body feels a gentle prickling and warmth, caused by the intensification of life within. The eyes become clear and bright, the skin takes on a fresh healthy glow, and every faculty—spiritual, mental, emotional, and physical—becomes enhanced to a considerable degree.

If there are any functional disturbances in any organ or limb, this is the moment when the attention should be directed and focused on that part. The result of this focus of attention directs a flow of energy over and above the general equilibrium just established. The diseased organ becomes bathed in a sea of light and power. Diseased tissue and diseased cells, under the stimulus of such power, become gradually broken down and ejected from the personal sphere. The revitalized bloodstream is then able to send to that spot new nourishment and new life so that new tissue, fiber, cells, etc., can easily be built up. In this way, health is restored by the persistent concentration there of the divine power.

When this is carried on for a few days in the case of superficial ailments, and for months in the event of chronic and severe troubles, all symptoms may successfully be banished without others coming to take their place. There is no suppression of symptoms; the result of these methods is elimination of the disease.

Even mental and emotional problems may be effectively dealt with by using these techniques, for the currents of force arise from the deepest strata of the subconscious mind, where mental and emotional neuroses have their origin and where they lock up nervous energy, preventing spontaneous and free expression of the psyche. The upwelling of vital forces through the entire system dissolves the crystallizations and armored barriers that divide the various strata of psychic function.

Where organic disease is the problem to be attacked, the procedure to be followed is slightly different—and one should still be under the care of a competent physician. In this instance a considerably stronger current of force is necessary, in order to dissolve any abnormalities or lesions and be sufficient to set in motion the systemic and metabolic activities to construct new tissue and cellular structure.

To fulfill these conditions in an ideal sense, it is very helpful to have a second person to assist, so that his or her vitality may be added to that of the sufferer in order to overcome the condition. A useful technique—one that my experience has discovered to be supremely successful, and one that any student can adopt—is first of all to relax completely every tissue throughout the body before attempting the Middle Pillar technique. The patient is placed in a highly relaxed state by first simply becoming aware of every neuromuscular tension. Consciousness is then able to eliminate tension and induce a relaxed state of that muscle or limb.

I have found that spinal manipulation and massage, with deep kneading, is a very useful preliminary, for in this way an enhanced circulation of the blood and lymph is produced—and, from the physiological point of view, half the battle is won.

Once a suitable degree of relaxation is obtained, the patient's feet are crossed over the ankles and the patient's fingers interlaced so that they rest lightly over the solar plexus. The operator or healer then sits on the right side of the person if the patient is right-handed—and on the left for a left-handed patient—and places his or her right hand gently on the solar plexus under the patient's intertwined hands, and his or her left hand on the patient's head. A form of rapport is established at once, and within a few minutes a free circulation of magnetism and vitality is set up, easily discernable by both patient and healer.

The patient's attitude should be one of absolute receptivity to the incoming force—this will be automatic if the patient has unwavering confidence and faith in the operator's integrity and ability. Silence and quiet should be maintained for a short while; then the operator silently performs the practice of the Middle Pillar, still maintaining physical contact with the patient.

The healer's awakened spiritual centers act on the patient by sympathy. A similar awakening is introduced within the patient's sphere, whose centers eventually begin to operate and throw a stream of energy into his or her system. Even when the operator does not vibrate the divine names audibly, the power flowing through his or her fingers sets up an energy that produces healing activity within the patient, whose psycho-spiritual centers are sympathetically stirred into the active assimilation and projection of force so that, without any conscious effort on the patient's part, his or her sphere is invaded by the divine power of healing and life.

When the operator arrives at the circulation stage, the operator employs his or her visualizing faculty, a veritable magical power indeed, so that the augmented currents of energy flow not only through his or her own sphere but through that of the patient as well. The nature of this rapport now begins to undergo a subtle change. Whereas formerly there existed close sympathy and a harmonious frame of mind, mutually held, during and after the circulations there is an actual union and interblending of the two energy fields. They unite to form a single continuous sphere as the interchange and transference of vital energy proceeds. The healer—or the healer's subconscious psyche or spiritual self—is able to divine exactly what potential the projected current should be, and precisely where it should be directed.

A number of these treatments incorporating the cooperation and training of the patient in the use of mental methods should certainly go far in alleviating the original condition. If necessary, medical and manipulative methods may usefully be combined with the mental methods described to facilitate and hasten the cure.

Although I have stressed healing of physical ills, it cannot be insisted upon too strongly that this method is suitable for application to a host of other problems. This technique will be found adequate for all other situations which may come before the student—whether it be a problem of poverty, character development, social or marital difficulties—in fact any other type of problem one has.

4

Tuning Ourselves to the Infinite

"We can tune ourselves to the infinite . . . through the mechanism of lighting up our inner centers, our own built-in receiver."

Repetition is often invaluable both in teaching and in learning new subjects, so some recapitulation of the various processes involved in the Middle Pillar practice will help to clarify some of the issues. And I would like to add a further consideration that will help to render the entire method more effective, and lift it to a higher plane of spiritual understanding and achievement. This final step will enable the student to call into operation dynamic factors within the human psyche which will aid in the production of the desired results.

The first step, as we have seen, is a psychophysical exercise. The student must learn how to relax, how to loosen the chronic grip of neuromuscular tensions in his or her body. Every involuntary tension in any group of muscles or tissues in any area of the body must be brought within the scope of conscious awareness. Awareness is the magical key by which such tension may literally be melted away and dissolved.

Only a little practice is necessary for this, and skill is very quickly and easily obtained. As physical relaxation is achieved, the mind itself in all its departments and ramifications undergoes a similar relaxation.

Physical inflexibility and psychic tension are the great barriers to realizing the omnipresence of the body of God. They actually prevent one from becoming aware of the everpresence of the life-force, the dependence of the mind upon—and even its ultimate identity with—the Universal Mind, the collective unconscious. When the mind's petty barriers are eliminated, and life flows through its extensive organization, we become conscious of the dynamic principle pervading and permeating all things. This step is without question the all-important phase in the application of these psycho-spiritual techniques.

Once having become aware of this, the logical procedure is to awaken the inner spiritual centers that can handle, as it were, this high-voltage power and transform it into a useable human quality. Possibly the easiest way to conceive of this is to liken the spiritual part of us to a radio receiver. A receiver must first of all be connected to a power source before it will work. Once power is flowing through it, then the rest of the intricate mechanism is able to come into operation.

So also with us: We can tune ourselves to the infinite more readily through the mechanism of lighting up our inner centers, our own built-in receiver. When the receiver is operative, then the divine current can flow through it in various ways, until both body and mind become powerfully vitalized and strengthened with spiritual energy.

But all this is merely preparatory. The radio may have power flowing through it, and all the equipment in perfect operating condition—but what do we want to do with it? So also with us.

Perhaps sickness is present. Or we need

money. Or we have undesirable moral or mental traits—or what not. We can elevate our minds by utilizing this energy, so that the desire of our heart automatically realizes itself with practically no effort at all.

The wish, the heart's desire, the goal to be reached, must be held firmly in mind, vitalized by divine power, and propelled forward into the universe by the fiery intensity of all the emotional exaltation we are capable of. Prayer is therefore indispensable. Prayer, not merely as a petition to some God outside of us somewhere, but prayer conceived as the spiritual and emotional stimulus calculated to bring about an identification with or realization of our own Godhead.

Prayer, sincerely undertaken, will mobilize all the qualities of the self, and the inner fervor that it awakens will reinforce the work previously done. Prayer renders success an almost infallible result. For in such a case, success comes not because of one's own human effort, but because God brings about the result. The fervor and the emotional exaltation enable one to realize the divinity within, which is the spiritual factor that brings our desires to immediate and complete fulfillment.

But I question whether prayer of the quiet, unemotional variety has any value at all here. This cold-blooded petitioning finds no place within the highest conceptions of spiritual achievement. An ancient metaphysician once said, "*Inflame thyself with prayer.*" Here is the secret. We must pray so that the whole of our being becomes aflame with a spiritual intensity before which nothing can stand. All illusions and all limitations fade away utterly before this fervor. When the soul literally burns up, then spiritual identity with God is attained. Then the heart's desire is accomplished without effort—because God does it. The wish becomes fact—objective, phenomenal fact, for all to see.

What prayers, then, should be employed to lift the mind to this intensity, to awaken the emotional fervor so that one can "inflame thyself in praying"? This is a problem to be solved by each one of us for ourselves. Every one of us has some idea about prayer which, when sustained, will inflame us to inward realization. Some use a poem that has always had the effect of exalting them. Others use the Lord's Prayer, or the Twenty-third Psalm—and so on for all possible types of people. I personally prefer the use of some archaic hymns known as invocations, but which are prayers nonetheless, and which certainly have the desired effect upon me of arousing the necessary emotional potential. In the hope that these might be useful to others, I include here a couple of these prayers, the first one being composed of short verses from various scriptures.

"I am the Resurrection and the Life. Whosoever believeth on me though he were dead, yet shall he live, and whosoever liveth and believeth on me shall have everlasting life.

"I am the First, and I am the Last. I am He that liveth and was dead—but behold! I am alive for evermore, and hold the keys of hell and death. For I know that my Redeemer liveth and that he shall stand at the latter day upon the Earth.

"I am the Way, the Truth, and the Life. No man cometh unto the Father but by me. I am the Purified. I have passed through the gates of darkness into Light. I have fought upon earth for good. I have finished my work. I have entered into the invisible.

"I am the Sun in his rising, passed through the hour of cloud and of night. I am Amoun, the Concealed One, the opener of the day. I am Osiris Onnophris, the Justified One, the Lord of Life triumphant over death. There is no part of me which is *not* of the Gods. I am the Preparer of the Pathway, the Rescuer unto the Light. Let the White Light of the Divine Spirit descend!"

The second prayer is rather different from the above, although both have a similar personal effect when slowly repeated, meditated upon, and felt intensely. This second prayer consists of two parts—the first one being a sort of petition of the higher divine Self, while the second part signifies the realization of identity with it.

> "Thee I invoke, the Bornless One. Thee that didst create the Earth and the Heavens. Thee that didst create the Night and Day. Thee that didst create the Darkness and the Light. Thou art Man-Made-Perfect, whom no man hath seen at any time. Thou art God and very God. Thou has distinguished between the Just and the Unjust. Thou didst make the female and the male. Thou didst produce the seed and the fruit. Thou didst form men to love one another and to hate one another. Thou didst produce the moist and the dry, and That which nourisheth all created things."

The second half should only follow after a long pause, in which one attempts to realize just what it is that the prayer has asserted, and that it is raising the mind to an appreciation of the hidden secret Godhead within, which is the creator of all things.

> "This is the Lord of the Gods. This is the Lord of the Universe. This is He, who hav-

ing made voice by his commandment is Lord of all things, king, ruler, and helper. Hear me, and make all spirits subject unto me, so that every spirit of the firmament and of the ether, upon the earth and under the earth, on dry land and in the water, of whirling air, and of rushing fire, and every spell and scourge of God the Vast One may be made obedient unto me.

"I am He, the Bornless Spirit, having sight in the feet, strong, the immortal Fire. I am He, the Truth, I am He who hates that evil should be wrought in the world. I am He that lighteneth and thundereth. I am He from whom is the shower of the Life of Earth. I am He whose mouth ever flameth. I am He, the begetter and manifester unto the Light. I am He, the Grace of the World. The Heart Girt with a Serpent is my Name."

These sample prayers are suggestive only and are to be used or rejected, as each student feels fit. They operate for me—they may operate in the case of other students, or not, as the case may be.

5

Other Uses of the Technique

"By stimulating our centers within and then formulating clearly and vividly our demands upon the universe, we are capable of attracting almost anything we require. . . ."

As I have suggested before, there are other uses of the Middle Pillar technique, quite apart from therapy. Enterprising students will divine their own uses for it.

It may be for various reasons that certain necessities of life, either physical or spiritual, have been denied one—with a subsequent sense of frustration and a limiting effect on character. Frustration always has a depressing and inhibitory effect on the human mind, producing indecision, inefficiency, and inferiority.

There is no real necessity why there should be any undue frustration and inhibition in our lives. A certain amount is no doubt inevitable. As long as we remain human it is quite certain that in some measure we are likely to be thwarted in our efforts to fully express the inner self, and consequently experience some degree of frustration. But any abnormal measure or persistent sense of thwarting and frustration may be dealt with and, by these mental and spiritual methods, eliminated.

First of all, an understanding of life is essential, and an unconditional acceptance of everything in life and every experience that may come one's way. With understanding comes a love of life and living, for love and understanding are one and the same. It also fosters the determination to no longer frustrate natural processes, but by acceptance to cooperate with nature.

The methods of spiritual and mental culture have long held out hope that these inhibitory conditions may be alleviated. Poverty of estate as well as of idea is a life condition that these techniques have always proven to be amenable to treatment.

The usual method is one of such deep and prolonged reflection upon just that mental stimulus, moral quality, or material thing that is wanted, that the idea of the need sinks into the so-called subconscious mind. If the barriers leading to the subconscious are penetrated so that the subconscious accepts the idea of the need, then, so it is said, sooner or later life will inevitably attract to one those things required.

But, as with all therapeutic methods, there are so many instances where, despite close adherence to the prescribed techniques, success is not forthcoming. It is my feeling and belief that they fail for very much the same reasons that their healing efforts fail: because there is not true understanding of the interior psychodynamic mechanism whereby such effects can be produced. There is no appreciation of the methods by which the dynamic nature of the subconscious can be stimulated so that the human personality becomes transformed into a powerful magnet attracting to itself whatever it truly desires or is necessary to its welfare.

Some people question whether this procedure is morally defensible. The answer is brief: Whatever faculties we have are meant to be used, and used both for our own advantage and that of others. If we are in a state of constant mental friction, emotional frustration, and excessive poverty, I fail to see how we can be of service either to ourselves or others. When we eliminate these restrictions and improve our mental and emotional faculties so that the spiritual nature is able to penetrate through the personality and manifest itself in practical ways, then we are in a position to be of some service to others. By stimulating the psycho-spiritual centers within and then formulating clearly and vividly our demands upon the universe, we are capable of attracting almost anything we require—as long, naturally, as it exists within the bounds of reason and possibility.

I wish to introduce here one other very powerful and effective element, one that borrows from astrology. I am not concerned here with astrology as such, merely that it is convenient to use its schema, its system of classification. I am not in the least concerned about arguing for or against the validity of astrology; I simply want to state that, from a practical point of view, the basic components of astrology are of untold value in that they offer a concise classification of the broad division of things.

Its roots are in the seven principal ideas, symbolized by the sun, moon, and inner planets, to which most ideas and things may be referred. To each of these root ideas there is attributed a positive and negative color, and a divine name for the purpose of vibration.

I propose naming the principal attributes as follows:

Sun: Power and success. Life, money, growth of all kinds. Illumination, imagination, mental power. Health. Superiors, employers, executives, officials. Positive color: orange. Negative color: yellow or gold. *Jehovah Eloah ve-Daas* pronounced *Yeh-hoh-vah El-loh-ve-dah-ahs.*

Moon: Changes and fluctuations. Women, intuition. The personality. The general public. Short journeys, moving to a new home or new area. Positive color: blue. Negative color: puce (a dark red). *Shaddai El Chai*, pronounced *Shad-di El Chi* (the *ch* is guttural, as in "loch").

Mercury: Business matters, writing, contracts, judgment, short travels. Buying, selling, bargaining. Neighbors, giving and obtaining information. Literary capabilities, intellectual friends. Books, papers. Positive color: yellow. Negative color: orange. *Elohim Tzavoos*, pronounced *Eh-loh-heem Tsah-voh-ohs*.

Venus: Social affairs, relationships, affections and emotions, women, younger people. All pleasures and the arts, music, beauty, extravagance, luxury, self-indulgence. Positive and negative colors: emerald green. *Jehovah Tzavoos*, pronounced *Yeh-hoh-vah Tsah-voh-ohs*.

Mars: Energy, willpower, haste, anger, construction or destruction (according to application), danger, surgery. Vitality and magnetism. Positive and negative colors: bright red. *Elohim Gibor*, pronounced *Eh-loh-heem Gi-bor*.

Jupiter: Abundance, plenty, growth, expansion, generosity. Spirituality, visions, dreams, long journeys. Bankers, creditors, debtors, gambling. Positive color: purple. Negative color: blue. *El,* pronounced exactly as written.

Saturn: Older people and old plans. Debts and their repayment. Agriculture, real estate, death, wills, stability, inertia. Positive color: indigo. Negative color: black. *Jehovah Elohim,* pronounced *Yeh-hoh-vah Eh-loh-heem.*

These very briefly are the attributions of the sun, moon, and planets under which almost everything and every subject in nature may be classified. This classification is extremely useful because it simplifies enormously one's task of physical and spiritual development. I'll give a few simple examples to illustrate the function and method of employing these correspondences.

Suppose I am engaged in certain studies requiring books that are not easily obtainable from booksellers. Despite my every demand for them, in spite of widespread advertising and willingness to pay a reasonable price for them, my efforts are unavailing. The result is that, for the time being, my studies are held up. The delay reaches the point when it is excessive and irritating, and I decide to use my own technical methods for ending it.

At certain prescribed intervals, preferably upon awakening in the morning and before retiring to sleep at night, I practice the rhythmic breathing and the Middle Pillar. By these methods I have made available enormous quantities of spiritual power, and transformed the subconscious into a powerful storage battery, ready to project or attract power to fulfill my need. This I circulate through the auric system.

My next step consists of visualizing the negative or passive color of Mercury—orange —so that meditating upon it changes the surrounding auric color to that hue. Orange is used because books, which I need, are attributed to Mercury, and I employ the negative color because it tends to make the sphere of sensation open, passive, and receptive.

Then I proceed to charge and vitalize the

sphere by vibrating the appropriate divine name again and again, until it seems to my perceptions that all the mercurial forces of the universe react to the magnetic attraction of that sphere. All the forces of the universe are imagined to converge upon my sphere, attracting to me just those books, documents, critics, friends, and so on, needed to further my work. Inevitably, after persistent and concentrated work, I hear from friends or booksellers quite by chance, so it would seem, that these books are available. Introductions are procured to the right people, and my work is assisted.

The results occur in a perfectly natural way—one is not to imagine that the use of these methods contravenes the known laws of nature and that miraculous phenomena will occur. Far from it; there is nothing in them that is supernatural. These methods are based upon the use of psychic principles normally latent within us, which everyone possesses. No individual is unique in this respect. And the use of these psychic principles brings results through quite normal but unsuspected channels.

On the other hand, should I desire to help a colleague who has literary aspirations but at a certain juncture finds his style cramped and the free flow of ideas inhibited, I should alter my method in one particular point only. Instead of using orange as before, I should visualize the aura as having a yellow or golden color, though the vibratory name would be the same.

Instead of imagining the universal forces to have a centripetal motion towards my sphere, I should attempt to realize that the mercurial forces awakened within me by the color visualization and vibration are being projected from me to my patient. If he, too, becomes quiet and meditative at the same hour, my help becomes the more powerful since he consciously assists my efforts with a similar meditation. But this need not be insisted upon. For, as shown by telepathy experiments, his own unconscious psyche will pick up automatically and of necessity the inspiration and power I have telepathically forwarded to him *in absentia*.

This system combines telepathic suggestion with the willed communication of vital power. The technical procedure is, as I have shown, extremely simple—even where employed for subjective ends. Suppose the realization suddenly comes to me that instead of being the magnanimous person I had imagined myself to be, I am really mean and stingy. Of course I could go to a psychoanalyst to discover *why* my nature early in life had become warped so that I developed a habit of miserliness. But this is a lengthy and costly business, and so much would depend upon the analyst and his or her relations with myself.

Instead, however, I might resort to the following technique. My first steps consist of those described before: rhythmic breathing, the light-shaft formulated from head to foot, and the circulation of force through the aura. Then, remembering that a generous outlook upon and attitude towards life is a Jupiterian quality, I would surround myself with an azure blue sphere while vibrating frequently and powerfully the divine name *El*.

It depends entirely upon one's skill and familiarity with the system whether the names are vibrated silently or audibly. But by either way, powerful Jupiterian currents would permeate my being. I would even visualize every cell being bathed in an ocean of blueness, and I would attempt to imagine currents invading my sphere from every direction, so that all my thinking and feeling are literally in terms of blueness. Slowly a subtle transformation ensues—as long as I am really sincere, desirous of correcting my faults, and if I attempt to become generous enough to perform the practice faithfully and often.

Similarly, if a friend or patient complained of a similar vice in him, appealing to me for help, in this instance I would use a positive color for projection. I would formulate my sphere as an active dynamic purple sphere, rich and royal in color, and project its generous, healing, and productive influence upon his mind and personality. Over time, the fault would be corrected to his satisfaction and his spiritual nature would be enhanced.

And so on, with everything else. These few examples will, I am sure, have shown the application of the methods.

It is not enough simply to wish for certain results and idly expect them to follow. Failure only can come from such an idle course. Anything worthwhile and likely to succeed requires a great deal of work and perseverance. The Middle Pillar technique is certainly no exception. But devotion to it is extremely worthwhile because of the nature and quality of the results that follow.

Once a day will demonstrate the efficacy of the method. Twice a day is much better—especially if there is some illness or psychic difficulty to overcome. After a while, students who are sincere and in whom the spiritual nature is gradually unfolding will apply themselves to the method quite apart from the promise which I have here held out.

Healing powers, freedom from poverty

and worry, happiness—all of these are emi-nently desirable. But over and above all of these is the desirability of knowing and ex-pressing the spiritual Self within—though it may be in some cases that this ideal is hardly attainable until some measure of fulfillment in other respects and on other levels has been achieved. When, however, the ideal is realized as desirable, then the value of this method will also be realized as supremely effective to that end.

About the Author

Dr. F. I. Regardie has been hailed as one of the most important figures of twentieth century mysticism. He was born in London in 1907, and first traveled to the United States in 1920. He wrote seventeen books between 1932 and 1972; his most voluminous work, *The Golden Dawn*, is a monumental study of Western magical ritual. *The Art of True Healing* is considered to be his most brilliant synthesis of the powerful effects of focused meditation.

He was a chiropractor as well as a writer, and later practiced a form of psychotherapy based on the work of Dr. Wilhelm Reich.

About the Editor

Marc Allen is co-founder and president of New World Library. He is the author of several books, including *The Perfect Life* and *Tantra for the West—A Guide to Personal Freedom*. A musician and composer, he has recorded several albums. Allen lives in Marin County, California, where he divides his time between writing, music, and the publishing company.

THE CLASSIC WISDOM COLLECTION
OF
NEW WORLD LIBRARY

AS YOU THINK by James Allen. Edited and with an Introduction by Marc Allen. October, 1991.

NATIVE AMERICAN WISDOM. Compiled and with an Introduction by Kent Nerburn and Louise Mengelkoch. October, 1991.

THE ART OF TRUE HEALING by Israel Regardie. Edited and updated by Marc Allen. October, 1991.

LETTERS TO A YOUNG POET by Rainer Maria Rilke. Translated by Joan Burnham and with an Introduction by Marc Allen. April, 1992.

THE GREEN THOREAU. Compiled and with an Introduction by Carol Spenard LaRusso. April, 1992.

THE MESSAGE OF A MASTER by John McDonald. Edited and with an Introduction by Katherine Dieter. April, 1992.